TELLING TINY STORIES

TELLING TINY STORIES

A Guide for Writing Real and Imaginary Lives

Michelle Dicinoski

Copyright © Michelle Dicinoski 2015
All rights reserved
Book design by Shaun Jury

ISBN 978-0-9943062-0-3

For more information, please visit
www.tellingtinystories.com.

Contents

Introduction v

How to Use This Book vii

Stories 1

    Dream, Connect, Record 3

    All Serious Daring 18

    Multitudes 33

    Open Doors 46

    Furrows and Traces 63

Extra Stories 83

Acknowledgements 103

Introduction

Many people would like to write down stories from their lives, but aren't sure how to go about it. "I'm not much of a writer," they say. "I wouldn't know where to start." This book is designed for non-writers and writers alike, especially those who don't know where to start. Using a series of prompts, it will help you to record fragments from your past and present, and to think about the way things were, or might have been, or might yet be.

Rather than asking you to write one long story about your life, *Telling Tiny Stories* encourages you to write many small fragments. After all, you live your life in a series of tiny stories, so why wouldn't you write it that way?

You might be thinking, *I'm too ordinary – who would want to read about my life?* This book is built on the belief that all lives are both ordinary and extraordinary, and that the most ordinary details about those lives – the rooms we have loved, the songs we get stuck in our heads, the clothes we like best – are sometimes the most intimate and telling. The prompts that follow will help you to remember exactly these kinds of details, and allow you to unearth memories of tastes and textures, sights and sounds, joys and disappointments.

Maybe you want to record stories from your life to give to your children or grandchildren. Maybe you want to record them for yourself. Or maybe you aren't sure if you want to record them at all – you'd just like to think about them. Whatever brings you here, I hope this book helps you to approach your past with a sense of fun, to discover and rediscover your stories, and to see them as the gifts they are.

Michelle Dicinoski

How to Use This Book

I don't believe in telling people how to approach a book, so these are more anti-rules than rules.

1. *Right and Wrong:* There is no right or wrong way to respond to the prompts that follow. For some prompts, you could respond ten different ways on ten different days and still be truthful each time. (You could also lie in each response and still be telling a kind of truth. But that's another story.)

2. *Audience:* You might want to record some of your stories for your children, or someone else that you care for. Even so, try to respond without thinking about an audience, or about what people will think if they read what you write. Thinking too much about your audience is the fastest way to stop yourself from writing. Write for *you*. Or for someone you'll never meet.

3. *Order and Pace:* Move through the book at the pace that seems right for you. You might skip some sections and return to them another day. You might even skip some altogether, or jump backwards and forwards through the book. Do what works for you.

4. *Do-it-Yourself Stories*: If you need more space for writing, or want to write extra prompts, turn to the back of the book to find blank pages.

5. *Difficult Stories:* Writing about the past can bring up difficult and troubling memories. Sometimes it makes us realise awful things for the first time, things that we didn't see when we were younger, for whatever reason. If you find yourself troubled by what you've written, consider taking a break. You might also want to talk to a friend or another trusted person.

Stories

Dream, Connect, Record

"I write to dream; to connect with other human beings; to record; to clarify; to visit the dead. I have a kind of primitive need to leave a mark on the world."

—MARY KARR

This book tells tales from the ordinary, extraordinary life of

―――――――――――――――――――――――――――――――――――――――

also known as

―――――――――――――――――――――――――――――――――――――――

who, if given the choice of any name in the world, or any name yet to be invented,
☐ would've preferred the name

―――――――――――――――――――――――――――――――――――――――

or
☐ wouldn't change a thing.

I was born in the year

_____

in a place famous for its

_____

_____

_____

Before I arrived, my family was made up of

_____

Once I arrived,

_____

_____

would never be the same.

Here is everything I can tell you about my first memory*—where it happened, who was there, and what I could see, hear, smell, taste and feel

---

* Here and elsewhere, if you're uncertain about the precise events, you could guess at what *might* have happened. "Maybe it was summer," you might say. Or, "My sister Kelly was probably there."

Some words I would use to describe myself

Some words others use to describe me

Some words that don't describe me at all

When I was seven my home was

It looked like

It smelled like

It sounded like

In this home, my favourite parts were

I wasn't supposed to go near

Today is the _____ day

in the _____ month

in the year of _____

Some things I am looking forward to

_____

_____

_____

_____

_____

Some things I am worried about

_____

_____

_____

_____

_____

A piece of clothing that I remember a family member or friend wearing when I was a child

What I am wearing as I write this

The bravest thing I've ever done is

It felt

Someone I adored when I was nine was

The thing I liked best about this person was

If I had to describe them so you could recognise them on the street, I would say

TASK

Trace the outline of your hand below. Then, inside the outline, write a list of some of the most striking things you remember ever touching or holding with your hands. What were they? How did they feel? What would you compare the texture to? Were they heavy or light?

The last time I danced was

The music I danced to was

I was dancing with

It made me feel

I have lived in _____ houses,

been to hospital _____ times, and

broken _____ hearts.

All Serious Daring

*"I am a writer who came from a sheltered life.
A sheltered life can be a daring life as well. For all serious daring starts from within."*

—EUDORA WELTY

Some things that I used to believe that I no longer believe

The worst thing anyone has ever said about me

The best thing anyone has ever said about me

Things that bring me joy

The best meal in the world

When I was younger, my answer would have been

As a child, I didn't like to eat

Now, I don't like to eat

If I listen very carefully right now I can hear

I thought I would never get over

but I did.

I thought

wouldn't affect me so much, but it did.

Three smells that I remember from my childhood

If the weather were an animal today, it would be

If it were a musical instrument, it would be

 **TASK**

Find a photograph that is significant to you in some way. Now describe the photo in detail, as if to someone who will never see it. What can you see in this photo? What is happening just outside of the shot? What is invisible in this photo? Why does this photo matter to you? There is space over the page for inserting a copy of the photo, if you like.

Someone I adored when I was thirteen was

The thing I liked best about this person was

If I had to describe the way they moved, and how their voice sounded, I would say

An object, tendency or biological trait that I inherited, but do not want

What I plan to do with it

My preferred way to get around is by

- ☐ foot
- ☐ bicycle
- ☐ train
- ☐ car
- ☐ bus
- ☐ plane
- ☐ wheelchair
- ☐ boat
- ☐ mobility scooter
- ☐ roller skates
- ☐ skateboard
- ☐ hitchhiking
- ☐ golf buggy
- ☐ this other way:

I like this method because

These prompts are fine, but what I would really like to write about here is

Multitudes

"Do I contradict myself?
Very well then I contradict myself,
(I am large, I contain multitudes.)"

—WALT WHITMAN

Three sharp things that I remember from my childhood

A time I felt very alive was when

When I think no one is looking, I

I have:

_____ siblings

_____ children

_____ musical instruments

_____ scars

_____ tattoos

_____ bad habits.

A very short anecdote about one of these is

I first felt really grown up when (or, I think I will feel really grown up when)

I wish I'd never

What happened during a perfect day that I once had

Someone I disliked when I was fourteen was

The thing I most disliked about this person was

If I saw them on the street today, I would

Something I made that I am proud of

I offer this piece of evidence that the world is remarkable

I offer this piece of evidence that the world wants to break our hearts

TASK

Below, insert a copy of a favourite recipe, whether it's one that you make, or one made by someone close to you.

I have worked at the following jobs (these can be paid or unpaid)

If I could do any job, I would like to

Open Doors

"There is always one moment in childhood when the door opens and lets the future in."

—GRAHAM GREENE

A person or event that has changed me, and how

My favourite piece of clothing ever

I regret ever wearing

If I could plan a weekend away with just my friends, and we could do anything and go anywhere, we would

The story I am scared to tell

I have lived in _____ towns and/or cities.

Places that I would like to visit

_____
_____
_____

My favourite place is _____

because

_____
_____
_____

My least favourite place is _____

because

_____
_____
_____

Things that seemed whole that I later saw were broken

Things that seemed broken that I later saw are perfect as they are

The song I always get stuck in my head

When I was fully grown, but not yet very old, I loved to spend my days

Things I fear about the future

Things I miss about the past

Things I miss about the future

Things I fear about the past

TASK

Go to the place where you store loose odds and ends. Maybe it's a kitchen drawer, or a dresser drawer, or a shoe box, or a trunk. Write an inventory of what you find there. If you like, you can insert a picture of what you find.

If I could make one lasting change to the world, it would be

Someone I adore now is

The thing I like best about this person is

If I had to describe them so you could recognise them on the street, I would say

A secret that I kept as a teenager, the people I kept it from, and why

When I fell in love with

it felt like this

and it happened like this

Growing up in my family felt

Furrows and Traces

"To write: to try meticulously to retain something, to cause something to survive; to wrest a few precise scraps from the void as it grows, to leave somewhere a furrow, a trace, a mark or a few signs."

—GEORGES PEREC

Advice I would give my younger self, if I could

Advice my younger self would give me now

My beliefs or traits that have landed me in the most trouble are

An example of this trouble is the time when

My dream house would have the following features

When I was eighteen, my worst enemy would have described me like this

My biggest admirer would have described me like this

The most irritating qualities people can have are

The most interesting qualities people can have are

Someone I've lost contact with, but would like to see again, and why

My worst trait is probably

My best trait is probably

Something I have lost, thrown out or given away that I wish I had back

Something I still keep that I should probably get rid of

Tomorrow I would like to

Three things I was passionate about as a child

Three things I was obsessed with as a teenager

Things my hands know that my feet don't

Things my feet know that my hands don't

Things I feared when I was younger

Things I fear now

If I were a superhero, my super ability would be

and my sidekick would be

Pets that I have had, by name and type (or pets I would like to have, because I haven't had any pets)

In a hundred years, if some person-of-the-future wonders about who I was, I would like them to know this one thing about me

If I could ask one question of some person-of-the-future, a hundred years from now, it would be

The problem with humans is

The great thing about humans is

Sometimes I like to imagine that

Important items that I have stored carefully for safekeeping

If all I could leave behind were one sentence, that sentence would be

Most of all, I am grateful for

Extra Stories

TELLING TINY STORIES

TELLING TINY STORIES

Acknowledgements

This book was completed with the advice and support of many people. I'd particularly like to thank Michael Bolger, Kylie Cardell, Antonella Casella, Amy Cross, Kelly Gardiner, Kate Goldsworthy, Elizabeth Hayes, Becca Hazleden, Benette Hibbins, Katherine Howell, Shaun Jury, Peta Mitchell, Renae O'Hanlon, Helena Pastor, Anna Poletti, Edwina Shaw, Elizabeth Stephens, Rosemary Stewart, Deb Thomas, Rachel Thorne, and Anna Zagala. And, as always, Heather Stewart.

www.ingramcontent.com/pod-product-compliance
Lightning Source LLC
Chambersburg PA
CBHW060529010526
44110CB00052B/2545